ZRJC
2/12

Young and Old

by Emily C. Dawson

amicus readers
A

amicus readers

Say hello to amicus readers.

You'll find our helpful dog, Amicus, chasing a ball—
to let you know the reading level of a book.

(A)

Learn to Read
Frequent repetition of
sentence structures,
high frequency words,
and familiar topics
provide ample support
for brand new readers.
Approximately 100 words.

 (1)

Read Independently
Repetition is mixed with
varied sentence structures
and 6 to 8 content words
per book are introduced
with photo label and
picture glossary supports.
Approximately 150 words.

 (2)

Read to Know More
These books feature a
higher text load with
additional nonfiction
features such as more
photos, time lines, and
text divided into sections.
Approximately 250 words.

Amicus Readers are published by **Amicus**
P.O. Box 1329, Mankato, Minnesota 56002
www.amicuspublishing.us

Printed in the United States of America at Corporate
Graphics in North Mankato, Minnesota.

Series Editor   Rebecca Glaser
Series Designer   Christine Vanderbeek
Photo Researcher Heather Dreisbach

Library of Congress Cataloging-in-Publication Data
Dawson, Emily C.
Young and old / by Emily C. Dawson.
p. cm. – (Amicus readers. Let's compare)
Includes bibliographical references and index.
Summary: "A level A Amicus Reader that compares
and contrasts young and old animals, showing how
old animals teach young ones. Includes comprehension
activity"–Provided by publisher.
ISBN 978-1-60753-001-5 (library bound)
1. Parental behavior in animals–Juvenile literature. 2.
Animals–Infancy–Juvenile literature. I. Title.
QL762.D38 2011
591.56'3-dc22

2011005586

Photo Credits
Kari Marttila/Alamy, cover top; Wayne HUTCHINSON/Alamy, cover bottom; Steve Bloom Images/Alamy, 4; Winfried
Wisniewski/Getty Images, 6t; ALASKA STOCK IMAGES/National Geographic Stock, 6b; Corbis Flirt/Alamy, 8, 20m,
22ml, 22br; Selecta/Alamy, 10, 21t; Лариса Курсина/iStockphoto, 12, 21m; Tierfotoagentur/Alamy, 14, 20m; Nathan
Blaney/Getty Images, 16t; Diaphor La Phototheque/Photolibrary, 16b, 20t; Stewart Cohen/Getty Images, 18; MICHIO
HOSHINO/MINDEN PICTURES/National Geographic Stock, 20b, 22mr; Vgm l Dreamstime.com, 21b ; Joe Potato
Photo/iStockphoto, 22bl; Arctic-Images/Getty Images, 22tl; Dušan Zidar/iStockphoto, 22t

1025   4-2011
10 9 8 7 6 5 4 3 2 1

Table of Contents

4

Let's compare young and old. Young animals are just born. Old animals take care of young animals.

cub

Let's Compare!

bear

6

A bear cub is young.
Mama bear shows him
how to fish.

robin

chick

8

A chick is young.
Mama robin brings
worms to her chicks.

10

A duckling is young.
Mama duck shows her
how to swim in the lake.

12

A kitten is young.
Mama cat licks him clean.

A puppy is young.
Mama dog keeps him
out of trouble.

Let's Compare!

A bunny is young.
Mama rabbit feeds
her milk.

18

A baby is young.

Mama feeds her milk.

Daddy gives her hugs.

Grandma rocks her to sleep.

Picture Glossary

bunny →
a young rabbit

← **chick**
a young bird

cub →
a young bear

← duckling
a young duck

kitten →
a young cat

← puppy
a young dog

Young and Old

Look at the photos.

1. Which animals are old?
2. Which animals are young?
3. Which animals belong together?

Ideas for Parents and Teachers

Let's Compare, an Amicus Readers Level A series, lets children compare opposites. Repetitive sentence structures, high frequency words, and photo labels provide support for new readers. In each book, the picture glossary defines new vocabulary and the activity page reinforces compare and contrast techniques.

Before Reading
- Ask the child about the difference between young and old. Ask: What things are young? What things are old? How do you know?
- Discuss the cover photos. What do these photos tell them?
- Look at the picture glossary together. Read and discuss the words.

Read the Book
- "Walk" through the book and look at the photos. Ask questions or let the child ask questions about the photos.
- Read the book to the child, or have him or her read independently.
- Show him or her how to read the photo labels and refer back to the picture glossary to understand the full meaning.

After Reading
- Use the Let's Compare activity on page 22 to review the concept of young and old.
- Prompt the child to think more. Talk about degrees of young and old, asking questions such as Who is an older sibling? Who is a younger sibling? Can you be both younger and older?

Index

Web Sites

Baby Animal Photos from National Geographic for Kids
http://kids.nationalgeographic.com/kids/photos/
baby-animals/

Names of Animals, Babies, and Groups from Enchanted Learning
http://www.enchantedlearning.com/subjects/animals/
Animalbabies.shtml